Table of Contents

Table of Contents 3
Introduction 4
1 - Normal Rights & Services 5
2 - Why I am Writing This Book 6
3 - Computer Controlled Access Freedoms 7
4 - Cost Awareness 8
5 - "How Would Segmentation Work?" 9
6 - "The Intensity of Density" 11
7 - Freeing Up Correctional Officers 12
8 - One Idea 14
9 - What's the Process 17
10 - An Opportunity For Staff Also 19
11 - Staff Productivity & Opportunity 20
12 - Prisoner Rewards 23
13 - Progressive Segmentation Careers 24
14 - Thank You 25
15 - Don't Worry Ever 26
16 - Resource List 27
17 - Angels Please Prayers 30
18 - Private Channeling 31
19 - Reverend Mike Wanner 33

Introduction

I have written about Access Control and many others ideas. My writings endeavor to keep the status quo safe and stable while adding optional improvements to the system.

That book invites the rethinking of prison flows and the way it happens every day in any one of the 6,000+ facilities in America alone.

When we control access, we can reduce possibilities for conflicts that help no one. We can look at what is appropriate for one particular facility at a time.

No elaborate master computer systems needed to replace the current methods but enhanced services, safety, security, and progress can grow out of peace and harmony and perseverance and refined access controls.

Prison Segmentation for Prisoner Guards and Freedoms

Rev. Mike Wanner

Copyright
Rev. Mike Wanner
January 28, 2018

Selected Images Used by License

1 - Normal Rights & Services

If you have been in prison any length of time, you know the normal at your facility and how to get into or stay out of trouble. Please assume that in addition to the normal that you see, there could be optional activities added when segmentation is included that could provide you with additional freedoms on time by time basis.

The optional activities could be considered after a peaceful segmentation application is implemented. The proposals that might be most likely to succeed would be the ones that are not self-serving but are laden with the potential to upgrade the cost-effectiveness and quality of life for the entire facility that you call home.

Over time participants could get creative and want to share progressively better options. As long as peaceful coexistence prevails, alternatives could be appropriately proposed, considered, tweaked and implemented when the focus is on efficiency and holistic, an inclusive expansion that includes taxpayers, administration, staff, and residents.

A vital component of this effort could be to require an option for all to request standard care at any given time. A default deactivation plan could be built into the system.

2 - Why I am Writing This Book

Every day is new, and we need the new possibilities that did not exist the previous day. Let's talk about a preplan, communication and structure to reshape flows with more freedom, more security, and less risk.

Let us help develop a working plan. All of this takes time so let's consider steps that allow a lot more independence. I hope that you can find options that bring peace, security, and flow.

This book is intended as a conversation starter because the rigidity of thinking needs to be redirected to more benefits at minimal risk for the whole system. The right resources at the right place at the right time can maximize safety for prison staff and prisoners while being economical for the bill payers we know as taxpayers.

I will put in Chapter 3 Dialogue 48 titled *Computer Controlled Access Freedoms* from my Dialogue Series Book and then develop a creative manpower plan to support that idea.

3 - Computer Controlled Access Freedoms
[Dialogue 48]

There could be a discussion about computer activated access freedoms that could be programmed to accommodate a variety of safety and security concerns to selectively isolate or free prisoner individuals or groups while still maintaining an equally fair balance.

Computerized access systems could be initiated to keep amicable residents, and less than friendly residents in Correctional Officer recommended patterns so that potential conflicts could be minimized.

Residents could come and go with more freedom, and that can have a tendency for individuals to self-balance their movements. If there were patterns established or keypads in cells to request access, prisoners might move ahead of or behind individuals or groups that may be less than hospitable to them.

Costs could be justified by safety improvements and conflict minimalization for both prisoners and employees. This type of idea could be implemented in multiple patterns with variable goals so that control and peace could be enhanced.

Changing times to accommodate preferences may sound extravagant for prison, but the minimalization of potential conflict situations could be a cost control system to eliminate trouble. Size limited group progressions within multiple progress paths could be lifesaving during any group challenge to authority.

4 - Cost Awareness

The invitation is to look at everything from a cost awareness perspective as that may just be the necessary component to receive the support of the administration.

Prisoner movement can involve a lot of staff time and prove physically vulnerable. Prisoner guards who have no physical contact with other prisoners could insulate the staff from harm while providing more freedom for the other prisoners.

Many prisons throughout the country have difficulty employing enough staff because of the vulnerability inherent in old facilities. When the prisoners outnumber the guards, there are risks to:

1. All the Guards
2. All the Prisoners
3. All the Guard's Lives
4. All the Prisoner's Lives
5. All the Guard's Families (What hurts their loved one hurts them)
6. All the Prisoner's Families (What hurts their loved one hurts them)
7. Administration's Performance
8. Administration's Budget
9. All the Owner Agency's Budgets
10. All the Owner Agency Taxpayers
11. All the Owner Agency's Ability To Govern
12. All the Prisoners sentence schedules

5 - "How Would Segmentation Work?"
{From chapter 14 in *Prison Segmentation for Safety*}

"Over time and in a progressive way that avoids capital costs, space can be reallocated to align utility with enhanced function. I used the idea of shifts that hospitals and airports use above to begin an example of timed functionality.

The idea is to provide opportunities to spread people out and improve possibilities for all. For most of the residents, things could stay pretty similar for awhile unless someone wanted to step up and out on a path of making things better for everybody.

Every great accomplishment starts with unusual ideas of things or new uses for different applications. Inventors of all kinds and visionaries go through a lot to bring us breakthroughs and are frequently not well rewarded.

Prisoners may have a more immediate reward in that the creation of a segmentation proposal could be solely in the use of thinking and dreaming and bringing alive faith or hope even if the experience is fleeting. Prison may be off-putting boring to many, and that may have something to do with the playground like competitions that can trigger trouble.

Even brain surgeons can find life boring when they are only doing the same things the same way in the same place every day just like the day before. Life can be fun. Fresh, dynamic and startlingly unpredictable aspects can add to the fun.

Have you ever noticed that eating the same thing over and over again is boring? Even gourmet restaurants can be annoying when it is always the same menu.

Life is vibrationally stimulated by new activities. When your sports team comes to your neighborhood and has tryouts for the kids, there becomes a new life of purpose that changes the vibrancy and joy of those who see it manifest.

Segmentation can allow diversity of many things to enhance the possibilities for the conceptualizing of a whole series of potentials that never before existed for any prisoners.

Segmentation can promote hope and potential and allow enough space for the manifestation of new life in the brains of old bodies. New thoughts can breed new realities that can eventually manifest into new good for many."

6 - "The Intensity of Density"
{From Chapter 3 in *Prison Segmentation For Mental Peace*"

"The Intensity Of Density Can Cause Enormous Stress"

11

7 - Freeing Up Correctional Officers

Correctional Officers have significant assignments, and parts of their jobs may not be as satisfying as possible. Standard operating procedure at our prisons may be more complicated and less productive than we might like.

The roles of correctional officers have evolved over time, and there is a lot that they do. Progress in many things is determined by little things along the way that is not seen outside of the internal decision sessions.

The goal of keeping prisoners from the citizens seems to be successful while prisoners are incarcerated. Rehabilitation is frequently reported as less than successful.

Unfortunately, most reports that I read are focused on blaming agencies for lousy performance, violation of prisoner's rights, mistreatment and a list of abuses and failures. Outside criticism may not be as productive as the critics intend as it can shift staff into a defense of self instead of service to the community and rehabilitation.

My books endeavor to avoid blame and focus on possibilities, but that message is slow to find listeners. This is my 49th book about prison possibilities, and I am hopeful that each reader offers the community many new ideas to process into change.

If we could remove tedious functions from correctional officers by assigning some basic tasks to prisoners, we could free up their time and their talents for work that can serve the community better. To do that, we need to open our minds to changes that could enhance the dignity and respect for both groups.

Redefinition of possibilities can serve us well in that regard. The way that things have always been done is not the end of the discussion.

Let us focus on goals that could achieve higher purpose and satisfaction. Optimal Employment and opportunity are worthy goals that can serve both prisoners and security officers alike.

Consider please if the reader and the community can conceive secure plans for realigning functions to allow:

1. Optimal safety for correctional officers.

2. Optimal safety for prisoners.

3. Reduction of non-beneficial interactions and challenges between correctional officers and prisoners.

4. Reduction of conflicts for all members of the prison community.

5. Opportunities for personal growth for all members of the prison community.

6. Proposals that can free correctional officers from tedious pursuits that maintain a status quo without an optimized plan.

8 - One Idea

Correctional officers are in charge of moving prisoners in a way that is as safe as possible. Prisoners may rarely get to participate in discussions about the way this is done.

We could start some dialogues about the way things have been done and what might be a better way to do things in the future. Discussion facilitators may find some value in starting with a brief invitation session seeking participation in the effort and suggesting written ideas for discussion at future meetings.

It could be essential to start the discussion with an overview that details a big picture of possibility. The steps to achieving the goal and the rewards for all can help frame all the options.

Efficiency at the prison can help all staff and participants in the program. A starting point might be ways to better serve the freedom of movement for prisoners by building in some flexibility.

What if we freed up the correctional officers to look at the bigger picture by creating roles for prisoners whereby they were the ones who had a function whereby they invited prisoners from one area of the prison to another in a controlled way. The view that I would like to see is the progressive development of access control paths within the jail so that many of the movements are more intuitive and less strict on a timeline basis.

Periodically throughout any day, people think to do different things at different times. At lunchtime, people are usually ready to eat, and encouragement will not be needed to go to the dining room but access will.

The most peaceful prisoner experience will likely be when obstructions do not block one from doing what they are inclined to do when they are motivated. Access available when motivated will not be judged by the incidentals of who pushes what button to allow access when one wants to go.

Of course, the idea of the fox in charge of the hen house comes up and a sense of inappropriateness with it. That warning inclination can be muted when the freedoms of access are limited explicitly to options that are set by the administration.

Ideally, we can have people doing what they want to do when they want to do it while maintaining a required level of appropriate order and control. Freedom of access can help keep the prison peaceful.

Access granted by prisoners can allow staffers to spend time on more productive efforts like coaching and rehabilitation. Ideally, we could start a whole new level of service to help prisoners, prison staff, administration, and taxpayers.

At the same time, we can create a whole new set of circumstances for prisoners. Prisoners with a little to a lot more freedom can begin to put their lives together in new ways.

Freedom has meant a lot to all who have chosen to create their own version of the American Dream. They have come from near and far to create new possibilities for themselves and their families.

I dream now of new realities for our prisoners because they and the country need new ways in which to stimulate change and rebirth. The prison crises across the nation are indications that we have been on the wrong path and now is the time for a change.

It starts with each person who will think a thought so please let yourself be the first to feel positive about the many things that are possible where you live.

The balance will always be needed so each proposal should include ideas of stepdown integration that acts as an automatic security stepdown breakpoint from the liberty provided. Care should be taken to keep as much progress as possible so that temporary setbacks will still be at points progressed to that is further on the task path than the original start point.

Avoiding lost progress can make little interruptions be less likely to disturb the peace and success experience of participants.

9 - What's the Process

The administration would need to supervise and approve the step integration design progressively to make this shift comprehensive and safe.

Proposals to:

1. A potential upgrade to the systems that are in place so that it is easily justifiable for expedient implementation.

2. Help Correctional officers and administrators know their strengths and vulnerabilities better than anyone else and design around for maximum benefit. (Of course, it would be a good idea to get second opinions along the way from affiliate facilities.)

3. Tarket as best one can the best places that can impact the most people.

4. Analyze the total job requirements for the correction officers in the position now and documenting each task.

5. Determining which tasks need to be handled by correction officers and which could be reassigned to trained prisoners that are trusted.

6. Determine the overriding automatic security over the task performance site.

7. Progress is detailing the initial site and the setup and implementation needed.

8. Request administration to evaluate and refine the process, the tasks and the benefits of the work accomplished.

9. Request administration to evaluate the time savings for correction officers and the value of going further.

10. Consider rewards to participating prisoners for taking the initiative for saving expense and helping to allow reallocating correctional officers productive efforts to benefit all who work and reside in the facility.

11. Consider other ways that prisoners can take the initiative to serve the facility and equip themselves with new life skills.

12. Evaluate the change in personal dynamics between the prisoners and the staff.

10 - An Opportunity for Staff Also

The task analysis described above will highlight not only the critical elements of the correction officer's jobs but all the steps that can be reassigned so that the productivity of the correction officers can be optimized.

As the staffers get attention, the administration can see value in reassessing the individuals and realizing that they can have more potential if the facility develops all their skills and enhances their position by supporting their career growth.

Total facility performance can be enhanced by star individuals that are motivated to reach their optimal levels of performance. In the process, staff and prisoners will attain a level of competence that can exceed all expectations and promote a community motivated to excel by their awesomeness.

Excelling is characteristic of high performance and diligence which can promote competency and authority which prevents mistakes and upgrades professional performance patterns.

When staff is treated well, and prisoners are treated well, the problems that grow from disrespect can die on the vine and institutions can be immune from the kind of criticism that has been in the news in recent years.

High-performance staff and high-performance prisoners can lead quite quickly to high-performance rehabilitation and reduced recidivism.

All these characteristics assembled together is a success.

11 - Staff Productivity & Opportunity

Labor costs are essential to management, but the quality of labor productivity should also be prominent in the discussion. The success described above can be enhanced by further understanding motivation.

It seems that in the past, rehabilitation success was less than prominent in the stories that reach the outside world. A component of what appears to be anchored in the transient nature of prison employment.

Prisoner containment seems to be more of the discussion about the label, tag, brand of the judgment than about the salvageable misdirected human inside the body who resides in the facility.

Of course, that could be easily reasoned if the prestige of the position that the staffers are in becomes more respected by the rewards of their toil that shows in the paycheck. The old expression something like - "what goes around comes around (anon.)", could be a good indication of the motivation for staff in some prisons.

Of course, it goes without saying that all 6,000 plus prisons in America do not lack in good personnel support. Facilities that have issues, however, may find their personnel policies are a right place to start.

The whole prison situation is about human dynamics for both prisoners and staff. This segmentation effort can improve opportunities for prisoners and staff and administration and taxpayers. Now, that's performance.

Human beings can be very complicated to understand at times, but they also can be very simple when approached directly and appropriately. Listening to staff members can make a remarkable difference in some organizations sometimes.

Money is not always the critical difference in productivity. Many people perform far better than required just because they were asked to participate in a meaningful conversation where their participation made a difference to others welfare.

Human resources can have a lot to do with the efficiency of a facility. To determine the motivations for employees or segmentation candidates, you may wish to ask some or all of the following questions:

Score the following from one to ten.

1. Doing routine work all day?

2. Putting One's Knowledge to work?

3. Do you like solving complex problems?

4. Freedom to make decisions without approval from a supervisor?

5. Do you like being micro-managed?

6. Do you prefer to know what the plan is?

7. Do you commend people who impress you?

8. Do you like being commended by senior staff?

9. Do you like Knowing there is an opportunity for promotion?

10. Present Pay Level?

11. Participation in a worthy effort?

12. How important are health benefits?

13. How important are dental benefits?

14. How important are vision benefits?

15. How important are 401(k) match benefits?

12 - Prisoner Rewards

A vital component of this concept is to change the status quo and create new options. Just like the program can enhance the awareness and motivations for prisoners and staffers, the realignment can begin to make a new reality by increasing the public image of both.

The money saved by the prisons through the realignment could be used many ways. I suggest that the following be considered as for rewards:

1. Tiered Staff Development.

2. Staff Enhanced Career Positions.

3. Prisoner Payments at higher rates than regular programs.

4. Prisoner Family Payments at high rates.

5. Prisoners Employment Options Development – Outside.

6. Prisoners Employment Options Development – Inside.

7. Enhanced Prisoner Family Time

8. Enhanced Prisoner Family Village Opportunities

13 - Progressive Segmentation Careers

While segmentation will spread prisoners out around the clock, prisoner guards can use stations within segments and eventually common areas to further disperse the crowd throughout as many locations as makes sense.

Each facility would need to create their own idea plans to progressively sub-segment, and the hope would be that there can be many opportunities for prisoners who are sub-segmented to feel safety and privacy. Of course, all sub-segments would be accessible as needed by the staff.

Segmentation needs to spread, and Prisoner Guard participants could be considered as ambassadors to step up their service while still in their sentence and step up their service income so that when they re-enter, they take with them a specialty skillset that can be used to get them employed right away.

Their skills will be able to help them pay the bills and get out and stay out.

The success will also give other prisoners hope for freedom.

Another option could be to provide some ramp up possibilities where released prisoners could stay for a while as residential employees who earn a wage after residential subsidy that allows them a little time to build some money to help them when they get home.

14 - Thank You

For Considering These Ideas

15 - Don't Worry Ever

Ever

It Does Not Help Prayer Still Does!

Resource: http://Create-A-Prayer.com

16 - Resource List

Distant Healing Sessions (or Join Mail List) – Write To mikewann@voicenet.com

Books by Rev. Mike at **www.Amazon.com:**

Veterans Healing Six Pack
1. *Trauma Healing Options for VA Hospitals: Help for Veterans to Own Their Healing and their future.*
2. *Trauma Healing Action Steps for Veterans: Help to Start Healing*
3. *Trauma Healing Action Steps for Veterans: Empowerment*
4. *Trauma Healing Action Steps for Veterans: Forgiveness*
5. *Trauma Healing Action Steps for Veterans: Thought Freedom*
6. *Tea for Veterans: Welcome One Home*

PTSD Power Pack:
1. *The PTSD Project: Turn Pain To Power*
2. *PTSD & Soul Retrieval: Putting One Back Together*
3. *PTSD & The Purple PAD: Calling all Scientists and PTSD Patients*

Angel Raphael Speaks Volume 1: Take Courage! God Has Healing in Store for You!
Angel Raphael Speaks Volume 2: Take Courage! God Has Healing in Store for You!
Angel Raphael Speaks Volume 3: Take Courage! God Has Healing in Store for You!
Angel Raphael Speaks Volume 4: Angels, Addicts, Alcoholics & Prisoners – Oh Yeah!
Angel Raphael Speaks Volume 5: Prisoners Caring for Alcoholics - Australia In Miniature Projects Intro
Angel Raphael Speaks Volume 6: Prisoners Caring for Addicts - Australia In Miniature For Addicts
Reiki Journaling from Japan
Reiki Is Alive: God's Great Gift
Four Parts to Healing
Distant Healing: We Are All Connected

Stress Release Energy Work: How To Cope
Does Reiki Love Heal Cancer?
Group Consciousness
Salute To Philadelphia VA Medical Center: Thank You
Reiki Transcript for Reiki 2 & 3 Channels: Dr. Usui Is That You?
God Bless Kindle & Amazon
Puppies Are Different From People
If Your Dog Dies
Toy Guns Are Obsolete
Great Spirit Made Children With Red Skin: AND
The Cage of Fear: Is Not Locked
God Made Children Red, Yellow, Brown, Black & White: Greet Each Child With Kindness
Emergency Medical Kindness In The Cradle Of Liberty: Big City – Cracked Bell
Angels Are Always Around Addicts and Addicts: Help Is Near Now! Invite It In!
Angels Are Always Around Addicts and Alcoholics: Volume 2 - Tools To Help Re-Light Your Life
Prison Jobs Now: Providing Care For Addicts And Addicts
Controlled Care Communities Concept
Prison Possibilities Dialogue Series: Concept
Prison Possibilities Dialogue Series: Volume 2, 3, 4, 5 Dialogues
Prison Possibilities Voluntary Exile
Prison Possibilities Corrections Coaches
Prison Possibilities For Mexicans: Is A Boat Better Than A Wall?
Prison Possibilities Family Time: A Reason to Thrive!
Prison Genius Pool: "So Much Genius In Jail."
Prison Possibilities Access Control: Prisoner Access by Request
Prisoner's Lawyers Can Save The American Economy: Make A Buck Doing It & ...
Prisoner Family Talks, Days, Stays & Vacations: Connecting Helps Healing
Prisoner Writing Projects: Write To Heal, Start Over & Reconnect
Prison Cell Clearing & Blessing: Clear Entities, Chase Ghosts, & Create Sacred Space
Prisoner Professors: Show You Are Aware Create Change With Care

Prison Reiki? Maybe Someday? A Gateway To Help Heal Prisons & America?
Judges and An Angel Rule On Possibilities: We Can Cut Sentences & Prison Costs
Ideas For Prison Wardens: Leadership Is Not Easy
Solitary Community: Could Community Support Cut Costs and Issues?
Prison Project Communications Team: Communications Can Change Lives
Motivating & Empowering Prisoners? Invite Prisoners To Find Their Motivation
Prison Segmentation For Safety, And Sanity, Security, Peace, and Space
Prison Segmentation For Security
Dowsing for Prisoners; Answers from Above
Ex-Prisoner Possibilities With Real Estate Investors
Prison Segmentation For Joint Ventures
Prison Segmentation For Your Rehabilitation: R U Ready?
Prison Segmentation For Family Villages
Prison Segmentation For Senior Prisoners
Prison Segmentation For Coaching Clubs
Prison Segmentation For Miracles
Prison Segmentation For A Prison Game Show
Prison Segmentation For Spousal Support
Prison Segmentation For Exit Contracts
Prison Segmentation For Sentence Segments
Penitentiary Edition Angel Raphael Speaks
Prison Segmentation For Overnight Visitors
Prison Segmentation For Lifer Purpose Plan

Little Books on Kindle.com by Rev. Mike:
English Medical History Questionnaire For Non-English Speakers
English Language Helper For Non-English Speakers
Wise Wonderful Women Are The Well Of The Family
Answers to Test & Research: Dowsing Power
Crisis? Reiki! Baby? Reiki!
Bible References For Healing
Angel Raphael Speaks – Prisons
Angel Raphael Speaks – Veterans
The Saint Off Interstate 95

17 - Angels Please Prayers

Addict's
Angels of Healing Selected
Help Me to Stay Directed
Come To Me From The Sky
I Am Ready to Succeed Not Try
If I Don't Invite You In
I Might Not Win
I Have Been Lost For Too Long
Help Me To Stay Strong

&

Alcoholic's
Angels of Healing On High
Help Me to Stay Dry
Come To Me From The Sky
I Am Ready to Succeed Not Try
If I Don't Invite You In
I Might Not Win
I Have Been Lost For Too Long
Help Me To Stay Strong

From

http://AngelRaphaelSpeaks.com/AAAAAAA/

18 - Private Channeling

Angel Raphael Speaks a series of free messages that are channeled through Reverend Mike Wanner for the Highest good and Highest Healing of all concerned.

Many questions arise about Reverend Mike doing private channeling, and he does help with that so e-mail him.

Reverend Mike is available worldwide as a psychic channel, emotional release facilitator, spiritual energy practitioner & teacher, and public speaker. He looks forward to meeting you soon!

Email - mikewann@voicenet.com 215-342-1270

PRIVATE SPIRITUAL READINGS/channelings or Spiritual Healing Sessions: Telephone or in person.

Rev. Mike is available for individual, intuitive one-on-one sessions with you, his Guide Family, and your Guides. He helps by offering clarity on emotional situations about your life, your purpose, your spirituality, and the release of stuffed emotions and cellular memory.

Connect to the love of your Guides today!

Contact Rev. Mike for an appointment.

Sessions available:

Spiritual Readings
Angel Channeling
Distant Reiki Healing
Distant Clearing of Stuffed Emotions
Distant Clearing Cellular Memory
Distant Clearing Energy Blockages
Distant Clearing of the Chakras
Customized needs
Mastermind dowsing responses to yes/no direction finding questions.

Rev. Mike is a facilitator of healing. He brings you and the Divine together so that you can align with the Divine and have a great time and a great life. All healing is between you and God, as it should be.

Go ahead and start without Rev. Mike. Visit his prayer site http://www.Create-A-Prayer.com. Take the first step NOW.

19 - Reverend Mike Wanner

Rev. Mike Wanner started his spiritual and ministerial studies with Reiki in 1993 and had studied seven styles of Reiki in the U.S., Japan, Canada, Denmark and Australia. He is certified to teach. He became certified to teach Integrated Energy Therapy in 1999 and co-taught the first IET class of the new Millennium. Mike began dowsing in 2001.

Ordained as a Metaphysical Minister of the International Metaphysical Ministry and an Interfaith Minister of the Circle of Miracles Ministry, Rev. Mike practices and teaches spiritual energy therapies in the Philadelphia Area.

Rev. Mike holds ministerial degrees from the University of Metaphysics and the University of Sedona. He is a Pastoral Care Associate at Jefferson - Aria - Frankford Hospital. He taught at the National Academy of Massage Therapy and Health Sciences.

Rev. Mike was a faculty member of the Medical Mission Sister's Center for Human Integration's School of Integrated Body/Mind Therapies in Fox Chase, Philadelphia, PA for twelve years.

Rev. Mike is licensed by the teaching of Intuitional Metaphysics to practice Spiritual Healing and Scientific Prayer. Mike is also a Prayer therapist.

Rev. Mike was elected in 2007 to the status of "Fellow of the American Institute of Stress."

In 2008, Rev. Mike became a practitioner of Coincidental Recognition as he incorporated the CoRe system into his spiritual healing practice.

In 2009, Rev. Mike trademarked a new healing process called Quantum Quatro! Subtle Energy System Support®.
In 2011, Rev. Mike joined the outreach program known as the Health Advantage Group.

In 2012, Rev. Mike became a Certified Professional Coach by The Master Coaching Academy and Joined The Personal Empowerment Group.

Prior to his spiritual, ministerial and coaching studies, Rev. Mike worked for Sears Roebuck and Co. while in High School and after graduation, until he joined the U. S. Air Force in 1965. He returned to Sears from Vietnam in 1969 and stayed until 1978. His final Sears assignment was as an efficiency expert in Methods - Operational Research and Development.

He volunteered with Burholme Emergency Medical Services from 1969 and is still a Life Member and Board of Directors Member. He started a private ambulance company in 1975 and worked professionally in the field until 2001 when he devoted his full attention to real estate investing, healing, coaching, and writing.

www.ReverendMikeWanner.com